SOUL DECREES FOR KIDS

SOUL DECREES FOR KIDS

BY: KATIE SOUZA

AND NISA LEHMAN

ILLUSTRATED AND DESIGNED BY
JAMIE LYN WALLNAU

ISBN-978-0-9992851-1-4

Printed in the United States of America

DEDICATION

This book is dedicated to my mom, Polly.
Her twenty-five year illness drove me to the feet of Jesus
for answers. The fruit you find here is just a tiny portion
of what I learned through the process.
Thanks, Mom. I still miss you every day.
Katie Souza

ACKNOWLEDGEMENTS

We are so excited and grateful to have worked with one another on co-authoring this wonderful book, Soul Decrees for Kids. We have been greatly blessed by the many wonderful people who worked very hard assisting with this project. Big love to the staff at Katie Souza Ministries for your support. Special thanks to Jean Mulquin and Genie Alley, for being great sounding boards to bounce ideas off of.

Big thanks to Carol Martinez and Anne Knight for our initial edit.

Special appreciation to Lalenunat Johnson for her many hours of editing, proofreading, and re-editing each version as we worked towards our final product.

Also, extra special thanks to our talented friend, Jamie Lyn Wallnau! We believe our children readers will enjoy the beautiful illustrations. Thank you, Jamie Lyn, for your energy, patience, and awesome talent in illustrating and formatting this book.

But, the biggest thanks goes to our Lord and Savior Jesus Christ. Thank You Jesus! You knew us before we were born. You protect and show unbelievable mercy and patience. You are our Rock, Strong Tower, Wheel in the Middle of the Wheel, our North Star, Beginning, and End. We love you and you are worthy of all our praise!!!!! Lord, bless this effort and every child that holds a copy in their hand. Allow each of them to not only read the messages, complete the activities, and say the prayers, but cause the words in this book - Your Word - to have an everlasting effect on their being. Lord, give them divine understanding and work fervently and effectively in their lives, we pray. Amen.

Soul Decrees for Kids
TABLE OF CONTENTS

Soul Decrees for Kids
TABLE OF CONTENTS CONTINUED

FORWARD

A few years back, I wrote *Soul Decrees*. The truths within its pages changed my life. I believe with all my heart that they will change yours and your children's too. Just like with Soul Decrees, we offer this book, Soul Decrees for Kids, with our fervent prayer that it will bring healing to the soul and enable children to have a strong foundation to begin living in daily victory.

From our own experience, we can tell you that the authority of God's Word will establish your victory and bring healing to every issue you face. We wrote this to give children powerful decrees that, when spoken, will establish healing in their body, family, and in every part of their existence. Declaring these scriptures will release an inflowing of healing power into the body and soul, and they will begin to experience healing in their relationships, supernatural health, and victory in every area of their life.

It is absolutely vital that God's people, including the kids, understand the amazing strength of His Word to heal our souls. Look at these points:

After Jesus had gone 40 days without food, Satan tried to tempt Him to turn stones into bread. Jesus answered, "It is written in the Scriptures, 'A person does not live only by eating bread. But a person lives by everything the Lord says.'" (Matthew 4:4 ICB)

The word "live" here means "vital power in itself and exerting the same upon the soul." [1] In this experience, I believe Jesus told Satan - the adversary of our souls - that the all-powerful Word of God can bring life to the wounded soul and thus thwart the devil's plans to attack us and make us sick, diseased, and troubled.

Also, the New Testament explains that Jesus Christ Himself is the Word. John 1:1-3 (AMPC) tells us,"In the beginning [before all time] was the Word (Christ), and the Word was with God, and the Word was God Himself. He was present originally with God. All things were made and came into existence through Him; and without Him was not even one thing made that has come into being." There is nothing the Word of God can't accomplish because the Word is Christ!

There are numerous scriptures that speak to the power of the Word. Here are just a few:

"He sends forth His word and heals them and rescues them from the pit and destruction." Psalm 107:20 (AMPC)

"This is my comfort and consolation in my affliction: that Your word has revived me and given me life." Psalm 119:50 (AMPC)

"By the word of the Lord were the heavens made, and all their host by the breath of His mouth." Psalm 33:6 (AMPC)

As we can see from these few examples, the same Word that created the entire universe can also heal us and give us life. Through this book, children will experience the power of the Word of God to also save, restore, repair, and heal every area of their lives including their mind, will, and emotions.

Further, James 1:21 (ICB) says, "So put out of your life every evil thing and every kind of wrong you do. Don't be proud but accept God's teaching that is planted in your hearts. This teaching can save your soul." The word "save" means "to save one suffering from disease, to make well, heal, restore to health." [2]The Word of God has the supernatural ability to heal our body as well as every wrong thought, free our will from bondage, and cause us to experience healthy, God-given emotions. We filled this book with scriptural decrees because they have the power to heal your soul.

Now, let's look at Job 22:28 (AMPC) where it says, "You shall also decide and decree a thing, and it shall be established for you; and the light [of God's favor] shall shine upon your ways." When you speak these scriptures, you are decreeing them. And when you decree healing scriptures over your soul and body, the Word will be put to work in your life, over your situations, and you will experience powerful success.

Lastly, God's Word is so sharp that it can cut and divide soul from spirit. (You will understand more about soul and spirit as you read this book.) We see this in Hebrews 4:12 (AMPC), "For the Word that God speaks is alive and full of power [making it active, operative, energizing, and effective]; it is sharper than any two-edged sword, penetrating to the dividing line of the breath of life (soul) and [the immortal] spirit, and of joints and marrow [of the deepest parts of our nature], exposing and sifting and analyzing and judging the very thoughts and purposes of the heart."

So, what does this mean for you? Many of the issues and problems that people deal with comes from their soul. However, most people don't know this, so they do not take action that can set them free. How many times have you wondered, "Why is this happening to me"? Well, as you speak or decree God's Word over your life, it's active, lively, effective power will cut through confusion, and get right to the wound that is deep in your soul, and heal it.

Parents and teachers, we pray you will walk your kids through this book, page by page. This book will empower them to know that God is there for them, and learn to speak God's Word over their lives to increase their faith, and have hope and victory in their lives. They will grow in their knowledge of the Lord, and of how to speak the life changing Word over their lives and the lives of others.

The Lord wants you and your child to "know the hope to which He has called you, the riches of His glorious inheritance" Ephesians 1:18 (NIV). Are you ready for your child to start this awesome adventure?

GOD MADE YOU

CHAPTER 1- DID YOU KNOW THAT GOD MADE YOU?

You made my whole being. You formed me in my mother's body.
I praise you because you made me in an amazing and wonderful way.
What you have done is wonderful. I know this very well.
You saw my bones being formed as I took shape in my mother's body.
When I was put together there, you saw my body as it was formed...
Psalm 139:13-16 (ICB)

God created every human being, and that means He created you too! He made you and put you together. Just like when you make a sandcastle, and push all the sand together with your hands to make a beautiful castle, God's hands were on you when you were made too! He formed every part of you and gave you the breath that you breathe.

Did you know that God put a lot of thought into the way He made you? Did you know that you are not a mistake or an accident, but a beautifully designed creation made by God? You were designed and created by God, just the way you are! And not only that, but God says you are made in an amazing and wonderful way. He likes how He put you together! You are amazing and wonderful!

PRAYER

Thank You, God, that You made me!
Thank You that You made me in an amazing and wonderful way!

What's Missing?

Complete the sentences below using the verse above.
Then, get it to stick in your heart
by saying it out loud to yourself.

God made my _____ being,
every part of me.
I am made in an _____
and _____ way.
God _____ me in my
mother's body.

GOD MADE YOU

CHAPTER 2- YOU ARE MADE JUST LIKE GOD!

So God created human beings in his image. In the image of God he created them. He created them male and female. -Genesis 1:27

God made you and every human being, to be just like Him! You are like a picture-perfect image of God!

That is what the Bible verse above means when it says you are created in His image. When you look in the mirror, you don't physically hop inside of the mirror and look back at yourself. You see an image of yourself in the mirror – a reflection. So, this verse means that when God was making you in His image, He wanted you to be a reflection of Him in every way. He made you to be like Him in the way that you look, in the way that you are, and in the way that you do things. He made you to be somebody that loves, creates awesome and beautiful things, does good, is full of peace and joy, and so much more!

PRAYER

Thank You, God, that You made me just like You!
I am a reflection of who You are!
I love others the way You love me!
I create amazing and beautiful things just like You do!
I do good things in this world, and do good for other people just like You!

DRAW A PICTURE OF SOMETHING YOU DO THAT REMINDS YOU OF GOD.
(How you love, help, or do good things.)

I AM MADE JUST LIKE GOD!

GOD MADE YOU

CHAPTER 3- GOD MADE YOUR BODY JUST THE WAY IT IS!

Yes, God even knows how many hairs you have on your head...
Luke 12:7 (ICB)

God made you just the way you are and knows everything about you, even how many hairs you have on your head! Wow! God gave you a body with fingers and toes, hair and a nose, and legs and feet. Did you know that God has a body, too? It talks about it in the Bible. It says that our Lord had hair white like lamb wool and as white as snow. (Rev 1:14) The Bible is such an amazing book to read because it tells us so much about God and about ourselves.

God has eyes too. He can see, just like you do, but even better! He sees you too! Have you ever thought about that? He has a mouth and uses it to talk, just like you do! God talks and He loves to talk with you! God also has ears that He hears with. Did you know that He hears you when you talk, when you laugh, and when you cry? One Bible verse even says we are in His hands. That means God even has hands Isaiah 41:10 (ICB). If we are all in His hands, God's hands must be much bigger than ours! Even though you can't see His hands, He does have them just like you do! He even has legs and feet, just like you do! Another place in the Bible says that He walks with us, just like a friend, and talks with us! Leviticus 26:12 (ICB) God is a lot like us. Aren't you glad that God made you, and gave you a body too?

PRAYER

Thank You, God, for making me and giving me a body!
Thank You for giving me eyes to see all that You have made!
Thank You for giving me ears to hear and a mouth to talk with!
Thank You for giving me legs and feet to walk and jump!
Thank You for giving me hands to hold and to help!

DRAW A PICTURE OF YOURSELF.

I AM WONDERFUL AND AMAZING!

GOD MADE YOU

CHAPTER 4 – GOD GAVE ME A SOUL TO FEEL AND LOVE!

Praise the Lord, my soul; all my inmost being, praise His holy name.
Psalm 103:1 (NIV)

...Love the Lord your God with all your heart,...
Matthew 22:37 (ICB)

God made you with a heart. Another word for your heart is soul. It is the part of you that thinks, feels, and makes choices. It's the way deep inside you part that feels happy and sad sometimes. Did you know that God feels too? The Bible is such an awesome book! It tells us how God feels happy and full of joy, but can even feel sad sometimes, just like us. God has a heart that feels like we do. One amazing verse in the Bible tells us that God thinks good thoughts about us. He has good plans for us – plans to give us hope and a good future. God thinks about us all the time! Do you think about Him? God's Word also says that God makes choices. He has chosen to love us, and to make us His children. He not only made you, but He wants you! You make choices every day too. Every day you choose to eat, to be kind and loving, and to play or sleep. God made you with a soul to feel joy and peace, think good thoughts, and make loving choices every day!

PRAYER

Thank You, God, that You gave me a soul to feel happiness and joy!
Thank You, God, that You think so many thoughts about me!
Thank You that You gave me a mind to think and imagine good and wonderful things! Thank You that You gave me a soul to make good choices, to always choose to love just like You do!

DRAW A PICTURE OF SOMETHING THAT MAKES YOU FEEL HAPPY.

GOD MADE YOU

CHAPTER 5- GOD GAVE ME A SPIRIT FOR HIM TO LIVE IN, SO I CAN WORSHIP AND PRAY!

God is spirit. Those who worship God must worship in spirit and truth.
John 4:24 (ICB)

You should know that your body is a temple for the Holy Spirit. The Holy Spirit is in you. You have received the Holy Spirit from God...
1 Corinthians 6:19 (ICB)

God is spirit. This means He is invisible which means He can't be seen, and He doesn't have a human body like ours. In fact, not only is He Spirit, but He can always be everywhere. And, do you know where He wants to be? Living inside of you! Did you know that when you believe in His Son Jesus, His Spirit comes to live inside of you? Imagine that! God living inside you! The Bible verse above says that you are God's temple. A temple is a place where God lives – a place where people worship and pray.

Did you know that you have a place just like that inside of you? It is your spirit. It is a place where God's Holy Spirit lives inside of you. It is a part of you that is made to worship and pray to God. God loves spending time with you. When you sing to God, thanking Him for His love and all that He has done for you, that is called worship and praise. When you talk to God and ask Him for help, that is called prayer. God is spirit and when you believe in Him, He gives you His Spirit to come and live inside you, and help you to make good choices. When you worship and pray, you pray with your spirit.

PRAYER

Thank You, God, that You are spirit just like the wind – strong and always moving!
Thank You, God, that Your spirit lives inside me when I believe in You!
Thank You that You give me Your Spirit so that I can worship You,
pray to You, and talk with You!

MIX AND MATCH

DRAW A LINE TO THE PART OR PARTS
(SPIRIT, SOUL/HEART, OR BODY)
THAT ARE BEING USED FOR EACH OF THE EXAMPLES BELOW.

Madison is eating an ice cream.

SPIRIT
(worships and prays)

Johnny is trying to figure out a math problem on his homework.

Amy is feeling excited because her friends are coming over soon.

HEART & SOUL
(thoughts, mind, choices, and emotions)

Gavin worshiped God at church.

Samantha felt scared when all the lights went out, so she prayed and asked God to help her.

BODY
(goes, does, feels, smells, sees, and hears)

Dallas is really happy when he swims with his friends.

GOD MADE YOU

CHAPTER 6- EVERYTHING GOD MAKES IS GOOD!

God looked at everything He had made, and it was very good...
Genesis 1:31 (ICB)

Our whole world was made by God! He created everything – the earth, the sun, stars, moon, water, trees, plants, animals, and everything in it – including people. After God had finished creating everything, He had something to say about all that He had created. God looked at everything that He had made and He said it was very good. Not just good, but VERY good! God made you, didn't He? That means He looks at you, and He likes what He has made. He thinks you are very good; you are awesome! Remember, you are made in an amazing and wonderful way. God put a lot of thought into making you, and loves you very much!

Think about yourself. What are some good things about you that God made? Look at everything outside and in all of nature. What are some good things God made in our world? Just look around. There are so many good things in our world like you, your friends, your family, all the animals, the wonderful stars and sky, beautiful trees and flowers, and the great big ocean. God has so many amazing and good things for us. That is for sure!

What's Missing?

Read the verse below, Genesis 1:31, and answer the following questions.

God looked at everything he had made, and it was very good.
Genesis 1:31 (ICB)

After God looked at everything that He had made, what did God think about it? _____

Who made you? _____

If God made you too, then after reading this verse, what does He think about you? _____

WRITE OR DRAW A PICTURE
OF SOME GOOD THINGS GOD HAS MADE.

God Made Everything Good, So What Happened?

CHAPTER 7- THINGS DON'T SEEM GOOD ALL THE TIME, BUT GOD IS WORKING IT OUT FOR GOOD!

We know that in everything God works for the good of those who love him...
Romans 8:28 (ICB)

Now, take another look at your world and ask yourself, "Is everything good all the time?" No, things aren't always good all the time, are they? Our bodies don't always feel good, do they? We sometimes get sick or hurt. Sometimes we feel sad and scared too; that doesn't feel good, does it? Sometimes we think mean thoughts or choose to do mean things. Sometimes others do mean things to us.

God made everything good and that is a fact! So why is it that things just do not seem good all the time? Well, something went wrong with God's creation. In the next chapter, not only are we going to see what went wrong, but we'll also see what God's plan was to fix it, and bring everything back to the good and perfect way He created it.

But for now, even though everything doesn't seem good all the time, we can trust that God loves us and that He works everything out for good! He loves us so much, even when things are tough. He will always take care of us, help us and give us what we need. He always has a plan to make everything work out for our good in the end!

PRAYER

Thank You, God, that You love me so much!
Thank You, God, that when things don't seem so good and I don't feel good,
You are always working things out for my good!
You will always take care of me, help me and give me what I need.

THINK OF SOMETHING THAT YOU THOUGHT WAS GOING TO BE BAD, BUT TURNED
OUT GOOD. WRITE OUT A PRAYER OF THANKSGIVING, OR DRAW
A PICTURE OF IT BELOW.

GOD, THANK YOU FOR WORKING THIS OUT FOR MY GOOD!

God Made Everything Good, So What Happened?

CHAPTER 8- SO WHAT HAPPENED? SIN HAPPENED!

All people have sinned...
Romans 3:23 (ICB)

In the last chapter, we learned that God made everything, and everything God created was very good – it was perfect and beautiful! When God first made everything, there was no sickness, no pain, no crying, and no sadness in our world. Imagine that! But the world doesn't always seem good and perfect like that anymore, does it? So, what happened?

Well, it happened way back in the very beginning of time, with the first people God made. Their names were Adam and Eve. God formed them and made a beautiful garden for them to live in. God enjoyed walking and talking with them in the garden that He made just for them. He loved Adam and Eve! God wanted to take good care of them, so He told them what was good for them, and what was not. God warned them not to eat from the tree of knowledge of good and evil. Sadly, Adam and Eve didn't listen to God, and ate fruit from the tree anyway. This is called sin. When we disobey God and don't do what He asks of us, this is sin. So, sin came into the world, and that's when things started to go all wrong.

God is love and He cares so much for us. Everything He says to do or not to do is because He loves us and doesn't want us to get hurt or to hurt someone else.

15

MIX AND MATCH

MATCH THE WORD ON THE LEFT WITH THE CORRECT BLANK IN THE SENTENCE ON THE RIGHT.

Listen

Disobey

God

Sin

Adam and Eve

1. _____ came into the world and everything started to go wrong. Things that were good started to turn bad.

2. Sin is when we _____ God.

3. _____ were the first people that God made.

4. Adam and Eve didn't _____ to God and ate from the tree He told them not to eat from.

5. _____ loves us so much that whatever God asks us to do is always loving because He loves us and doesn't want us to be hurt or to hurt anyone else.

God Made Everything Good, So What Happened?

CHAPTER 9- IN EVERY GOOD STORY THERE IS A BAD GUY WHO MESSES GOOD THINGS UP!

A thief comes to steal and kill and destroy.
But I came to give life—life in all its fullness.
John 10:10 (ICB)

Remember our story about Adam and Eve, how they didn't listen to God and sinned by eating from a tree that was not good for them? Why would they do that? This is a true story about the first people, and like in almost every story, there was a bad guy, an enemy. This enemy is Satan; he is the father of all lies. He hated God and wanted to steal from Him and destroy His creation. He came into the garden that God created, looking like a snake, to trick Adam and Eve into eating from the very tree that God said not to eat from, the tree of knowledge of good and evil. Satan said to them, "Did God really say that you must not eat fruit from any tree in the garden?" He tried to make them doubt what God said. He even said that it would be good for them to eat from the forbidden tree. He actually told them the complete opposite of what God had said, and they believed him instead of God! They disobeyed God, and ate the fruit of this tree.

The enemy, Satan, wanted to make Adam and Eve believe that God wasn't telling the truth, and he is still trying to do the same thing to us today. We may not see him, but he tries to make us doubt God too, so that we won't obey God and sin. Who do you think you should believe, God or Satan? GOD, OF COURSE!!! The good news is that God always tells us the truth. We can trust everything He says. God loves us so much; we can trust that everything He asks us to do is good and everything He asks us not to do is for our good.

PRAYER
Thank You, God, that You always tell me the truth! I can always trust You!
I can always believe what You say!

LET'S GET THINGS STRAIGHT!

Place the following events into their correct order by placing a number from 1 to 5 in the blank next to each event.

_____ Satan, the enemy, lied to Adam and Eve and said that it was good for them to eat from the tree of the knowledge of good and evil.

_____ God told Adam and Eve that they could eat from any tree in the garden, except for the tree of the knowledge of good and evil because it would hurt them.

_____ Adam and Eve did not listen to God, but listened to Satan instead, and ate the fruit from the tree of the knowledge of good and evil.

_____ Satan, the enemy, came to Adam and Eve looking like a snake.

_____ God created Adam and Eve.

God Made Everything Good, So What Happened?

CHAPTER 10- SIN HURTS EVERYTHING!

Sin came into the world because of what one man did. And with sin came death.
And this is why all men must die—because all men sinned.
Romans 5:12 (ICB)

It's your sins that have cut you off from God...
Isaiah 59:2 (NLT)

Did you know that when God created everything, He didn't want anything to ever die? Imagine that! When Adam and Eve disobeyed God, sin entered the world for the first time. This is when God's beautiful and good world started to become filled with evil, sin, pain, sadness, sickness, and death. This is when everything in the world started to go bad. God tells us to love people and when we don't, it causes people to hurt, doesn't it? Sin hurts our relationship with each other and with God. It can cause sickness and a lot of pain and suffering. Sin even hurts the earth and all of God's creatures. Sin also makes God sad, because our sin separates us from God. God is good, and He is love. He is light and full of life. When we are separated from Him, our lives get dark and full of hurt. God loves us so much that He wants to be with us all the time. He never wants to leave us, so that our lives are always full of light and love. He always wants to be with you, just like He was with Adam and Eve in the very beginning, walking and talking with them every day. Sin hurts everything, but don't worry. God loves us so much that He made a plan to make everything good again! He made a way to fix everything that sin messed up!

PRAYER
Thank You, God, that You always want to be with us!
Thank You, God, that even though sin hurts everything,
You made a plan to make everything good again!

LET'S CHECK IT OUT
WHAT DOES THE BIBLE SAY?

Sin hurts everything. Let's see what these verses say that sin does.

"Therefore, just as sin entered the world through one man, and death through sin, and in this way death came to all people, because all sinned…" Romans 5:12 (ICB)

What came to all people because they all sinned? _____

"It is your evil that has separated you from your God. Your sins cause him to turn away from you. And then he does not hear you." Isaiah 59:2 (ICB)

What happened because of our evil and sin?
_____
_____

WRITE OUT A PRAYER THANKING GOD FOR HIS PLAN TO ALWAYS BE WITH YOU, OR DRAW A PICTURE OF YOU AND GOD TOGETHER!
SIN SEPARATES, BUT THANK YOU, GOD, THAT
YOU WANT TO BE WITH US FOREVER!

GOD HEALS MY SPIRIT

CHAPTER 11- WHILE STILL SINNERS, GOD SHOWS HIS GREAT LOVE FOR US!

But Christ died for us while we were still sinners.
In this way God shows his great love for us.
Romans 5:8 (ICB)

We all have sinned. We all have done things that are wrong or unloving. Yet, even while we were still sinners, God showed His great love for us! God loves everyone – there is not one person in the world that He does not love, and that means you too! Sin brings death, but God wanted us to have life. So, He sent His one and only Son, Jesus, to earth to die in our place.

The Bible tells us all about Jesus' love for us, and all the things that He did. At Christmas, we celebrate when Jesus was born, because he came to earth for us. He did many miracles. He healed people who were sick, and He multiplied food when there wasn't enough. He taught people what love was. He also taught them all about God, His Father. However, the greatest thing Jesus ever did for us was when He paid the price for our sins by dying on the cross.

But thank God, He didn't stay dead! In three days He rose to life again! That's right! He was in the grave, but came back to life forever. That is the biggest miracle and the biggest act of love He could ever do for us. He loved us so much that He took our place, so that whoever believes in Him will not die, but live forever. What does this mean? See, when you believe in Jesus, He comes to live inside you. Remember how you have a spirit, the part of you made just for God? Well, when you believe in Jesus, His Spirit comes to live inside your spirit forever. Your body may get old and die one day, but your spirit will live forever with God in heaven!

PRAYER

I believe in You, Jesus! I believe that You loved me so much that You came to earth and died for my sins on the cross, then rose to life again. Thank You, Jesus, that because I believe in You, I will not die but have everlasting life! I get to live with You now on earth and forever in heaven!

DRAW A PICTURE OR WRITE OUT A PRAYER THANKING GOD
FOR ALL THE WAYS HE SHOWS US HIS LOVE.

GOD SHOWED US HIS GREAT LOVE FOR US!

GOD HEALS MY SPIRIT

CHAPTER 12 – WHEN I BELIEVE IN JESUS, I AM A NEW CREATION!

If anyone belongs to Christ, then he is made new.
The old things have gone; everything is made new!
2 Corinthians 5:17 (ICB)

We see this word "eternal" or "everlasting" a lot in the Bible, like in the verse John 3:16. "If we believe in Him, we will not perish but have eternal life," and in 1 John 5:12, "He who has the son has eternal life." Do you know what the word "eternal" means? It means "forever, ever-lasting, never-ending, endless, permanent, timeless." That means if you believe in God's only Son, Jesus, He brings your spirit back to life and not just for a little bit, but forever! Your spirit comes back to life forever; for all time! "But God's mercy is great, and he loved us very much. We were spiritually dead because of the things we did wrong against God. But God gave use new life with Christ..." Ephesians 2:4-5 (IBC). What an amazing gift God has given us - eternal life through His son Jesus!

Just think of your spirit like a light bulb. When the light bulb is plugged into electricity, it lights up and comes to life. When it is unplugged, there is no light and it doesn't work. Jesus paid the price for our sin, died in our place on the cross, and rose from the dead. When we believe in Jesus, His Spirit comes to live inside us, and it's like the lights to our spirit get plugged back into God, and they light up! Our spirits are completely new on the inside. We become a new creation, shining bright and full of life!

PRAYER

Thank You, Jesus, for coming to live inside Me forever and giving me light!
Thank You that my spirit is brand new and perfect because of You!
I am a new creation on the inside! I am full of light!

DRAW A PICTURE OR WRITE OUT A PRAYER
THANKING GOD FOR FILLING YOU WITH LIGHT.

I AM A NEW CREATION! I AM FULL OF LIGHT!

GOD HEALS MY SPIRIT

CHAPTER 13- HE FORGIVES ALL OUR SINS!

But if we confess our sins, He will forgive our sins. We can trust God. He does what is right. He will make us clean from all the wrongs we have done.
1 John 1:9 (ICB)

God is so good and loves us so much! He wants us to be loved and to love others. In fact, God is love! Everything God asks us to do is loving. If He asks us not to do something, it is because it would hurt us or someone else. It is really important that we obey what God tells us in His Word, but when we don't, that is called sin.

Even after we believe in Jesus and He comes to live inside of us, we still have times when we don't listen to Him and we sin. It is like with our parents or those that take care of us; we love them, but we may not always do what they ask us to do. The good news is Jesus not only died for our sins on the cross, but He also forgives all of our sin! What does that forgiveness mean? It means that God lets go of what we did wrong, He cleanses us from all the wrongs we have done, and forgets about it! Isn't forgiveness awesome?

All we need to do is confess our sin to Him and He forgives us. To confess just means to tell Jesus what you did wrong and that you are sorry. (Of course, we need to be truly sorry about what we did!) He is so loving that He forgives you and wipes all your sin away. As we grow with God and know of His love more and more, we will sin less and less, but it still happens from time to time. Anytime that you do sin, just take it to Jesus right away and tell Him you are sorry for what you did. He will forgive you and cleanse you from all the wrong, and love you!

PRAYER

Thank You, Jesus, that if I confess my sin to You and
tell You what I did wrong, You forgive me.
You make me clean from all the wrong I have done.
Please help me to do better next time! Thank You that nothing can
separate me from Your love! Thank You that I can always come to You
at any time, and You always welcome me and forgive me!

LET'S CHECK IT OUT
WHAT DOES THE BIBLE SAY?

But if we confess our sins, He will forgive our sins. We can trust God. He does what is right. He will make us clean from all the wrongs we have done. *1 John 1:9 (ICB)*

Read the verse above. What happens when we confess and tell Jesus our sins?

_____

_____

_____

_____

_____

_____

_____

_____

_____

CHEATING

DISOBEYING

STEALING

HATE

FIGHTING

LYING

TALKING BACK TO MY PARENTS

ARGUING

Jesus

GOD HEALS MY HEART AND SOUL

CHAPTER 14- THE BEST MEDICINES IN THE WORLD!
MEDICINE #1- THE BLOOD OF JESUS

But He was wounded for the wrong things we did. He was crushed for the evil
things we did. The punishment, which made us well, was given to him.
And we are healed because of his wounds.
Isaiah 53:5 (ICB)

...the blood of the death of Jesus, God's Son, is making us clean from every sin.
1 John 1:7 (ICB)

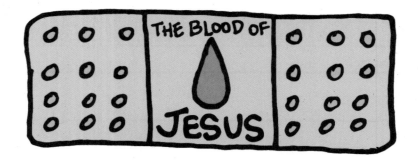

Jesus was cut, beaten, whipped, and wounded for us. There was a big enemy that
wanted to beat us up, but Jesus stood up for us and took the beating for us. Jesus
bled for us. He bled for you! If Jesus was willing to bleed and suffer for you, that
means that He loves you A LOT!

The blood of Jesus is a very special gift He gives to us – it cleans us! See, when we
sin, it hurts our hearts or souls. When we get hurt or wounded by falling and scraping
our knee, it is very important to first wash our cut, so that it can heal. Just like the
wounds on our body need to be cleaned up, our hearts need the same thing when
they are hurt. The blood of Jesus does this for us; it washes our hurt souls.

When we sin and are unloving, it doesn't feel so good, does it? It can make us sad,
fearful, or angry. Sometimes we can even get so worried that we get an upset
stomach. When we feel that way, our heart is telling us that it's hurting and needs to
be healed. Aren't you glad that God loves us so much that He gave us the best
medicine in the whole world? It's the blood of Jesus! The blood of Jesus washes
your heart when it hurts so He can heal you. God wants you to be completely well,
not hurting, angry, fearful, or in pain, but to be full of joy and peace!

PRAYER

Thank You, Jesus, for loving us and for giving us the best medicine in the world – Your blood! Thank You that Your blood washes my heart when I have sinned and You heal my heart when it is hurting. Thank You that the blood of Jesus is washing away any anger, sadness, worry, fear, or guilt that I may feel. Thank You for filling my heart with joy and peace.

LET'S CHECK IT OUT!
What does the Bible say?

But he was wounded for the wrong things we did. He was crushed for the evil things we did. The punishment, which made us well, was given to him. And we are healed because of his wounds. Isaiah 53:5 (ICB)

If Jesus was willing to be wounded and crushed for the wrong things we did so that we could be healed, how important do you think you are to Him?

_____
_____

When our hearts are feeling angry, upset, or sad, we know that our hearts are hurting. Jesus was crushed and He bled for us, so that we could be_____.

*…the blood of the death of Jesus,
God's Son, is making us clean from every sin.
1 John 1:7 (ICB)*

Fill in the blank. The blood of Jesus is the best medicine! It is making us _____ from every sin that wounds our hearts.

GOD HEALS MY HEART AND SOUL

CHAPTER 15- THE BEST MEDICINES IN THE WORLD
MEDICINE #2 - THE SUPER POWER OF GOD

God raised Jesus from death. And if God's Spirit is living in you,
then He will also give life to your bodies that die...
Romans 8:11 (ICB)

And you will know that God's power is very great for us who believe.
That power is the same as the great strength God used to raise Christ from death and
put him at his right side in heaven.
Ephesians 1:19-20 (ICB)

Jesus proved His love for us when He died on the cross for our sins. Yet, that wasn't all that Jesus did for us. Jesus didn't stay dead! He came back to life and walked out of the grave! He rose from the dead! Now that takes some power!! This is what the holiday Easter is all about; it is celebrating when Jesus rose from the dead and came back to life.

Not only did God raise Jesus from the dead, but His Spirit is living inside us, and that very same power that brought Jesus back to life is inside of us. Isn't that awesome? God's powerful Spirit, that raised Jesus from the dead, lives inside of YOU! That's right! This power is for us! It is to help us, strengthen us, and work through us. The word in the Bible for this power is "dunamis". Doesn't that sound powerful, like dynamite? This super dunamis power of God creates miracles and makes our hearts powerful to love and do good.

When our souls are hurt, they are weak and not very strong, but God's super power in us heals our hearts and makes them strong and able to love BIG. His super power in us gives us strength to be God's super heroes on earth, super heroes just like Jesus – full of love, joy, and peace, doing miracles just like He did.

PRAYER

Thank You, Jesus, that the very same super power that brought You back
from the dead and raised You to life is inside of me!
Thank You that Your super power is healing my heart and making me a
super hero like Jesus. This super power is making me loving, forgiving, and full of
joy and peace. This super power is doing miracles in my life!

DRAW A PICTURE OR WRITE OUT A PRAYER OF WHAT YOU WANT GOD'S SUPER
DUNAMIS POWER TO DO IN YOU.

GOD'S SUPER DUNAMIS POWER IN ME!

GOD HEALS MY HEART AND SOUL

CHAPTER 16- WHEN OTHER PEOPLE HURT ME!

Yes, if you forgive others for the things they do wrong, then your Father in heaven will also forgive you for the things you do wrong. But if you don't forgive the wrongs of others, then your Father in heaven will not forgive the wrong things you do.
Matthew 6:14-15 (ICB)

Unfortunately, most of us have been hurt by other people, whether they meant to hurt us or not. We are all sinners, and sin hurts. Since Jesus has forgiven us when we have done wrong and haven't deserved forgiveness, how can we not do the same for others? We forgive because we have been forgiven ourselves. It actually says in the Bible that if we do not forgive others, then we won't be forgiven. That is serious!

Has anyone ever lied to you, stolen from you, or hurt you? It is so important to forgive when you have been hurt. Forgiveness does not mean that what they did to you was right or that it didn't hurt you. Forgiveness means that you don't hold it against them anymore. You let go of the hurt or anger you feel and give it to God. We let go of the wrong done against us just the way that Jesus did for us. If we do not forgive others, we are sinning, and we need the blood of Jesus and His forgiveness again.

The blood of Jesus washes us from all sin, even the sin that others do against us. It hurts when others are mean to us. Our hearts can feel all sorts of emotions, such as anger, sadness, or being scared. The hurt in our souls can make us think mean thoughts or make bad choices to not forgive. Or, we might even choose to get back at them by getting even. The blood of Jesus and God's super dunamis power inside us can heal our feelings and give us joy and love. It can heal our thoughts and help us choose to forgive, and even be kind to those who hurt us. God heals our heart and soul when we are hurt by others. You can trust God to heal you, so that you can let go of the hurt and forgive.

PRAYER TO FORGIVE OTHERS

Dear Jesus, I was really hurt when_____ did/said this to me: _____. I forgive them because You have forgiven me. Thank You for Your blood - the blood of Jesus - that washes away my hurt feelings and the sins against me. Thank You for Your super power inside me that gives me love for them and helps me be kind.

DRAW A PICTURE OF YOURSELF FORGIVING SOMEONE.

WRITE OUT, OR SAY ALOUD, A PRAYER FOR THE PERSON YOU FORGAVE.

_____

_____

_____

_____

_____

_____

_____

GOD HEALS MY HEART AND SOUL

CHAPTER 17- WHEN I GET MAD AT MYSELF!

...The most important command is this... Love the Lord your God.
Love him with all your heart, all your soul, all your mind, and all your strength.
The second most important command is this:
Love your neighbor as you love yourself...
Mark 12:29-31 (ICB)

Have you ever done something that made you really mad at yourself? Have you ever hurt somebody you loved and felt really bad about it? We all have at one time or another. We know that God will forgive us if we ask Him to, and most of the time other people will forgive us too. But, I bet you didn't think that you might need to forgive yourself. Just like Jesus forgives you, He wants you to forgive yourself too! That means give whatever you did to Jesus and let it go; forgive yourself. Don't worry about it anymore! Trust that God can work it all out for your good because you love Him. Trust that God can heal whatever or whoever you have hurt too.

Trust that the blood of Jesus will not only clean your soul, but His super dunamis power will heal you and change you, so that you can do better next time. His power in you can make you more patient and loving. His power inside of you makes you kind, and helps you to make good choices.

Sometimes we get mad at ourselves even when we didn't do anything wrong. We get disappointed in ourselves when we missed the ball in a game or got shy and couldn't talk to a friend. God loves us and so we need to love ourselves too, even when we are not all that we want to be. We still need to forgive ourselves, let it go, and know that we are loved just the way we are. His super dunamis power in you gives you strength to try again, even though things didn't work out the first time. His power in you can give you the strength to do all things through Jesus.

PRAYER

Thank You, Jesus, that You forgive me when I sin, so I will forgive myself too.
I forgive myself for _____.
Thank You for the blood of Jesus that washes my heart when I get mad at myself, and thank You for Your super dunamis power, that gives me strength to love myself the way You love me!

INSIDE THE HEART, WRITE WHAT YOU WANT
TO FORGIVE YOURSELF FOR, THEN GIVE IT TO JESUS.

I FORGIVE MYSELF!
I AM LOVED!

GOD HEALS MY HEART AND SOUL

CHAPTER 18- WHEN BAD THINGS HAPPEN!

God is our protection and our strength. He always helps in times of trouble.
Psalm 46:1 (ICB)

Have you ever had anything bad happen to you, like an accident that caused you or someone you loved to get hurt? I was in a car accident once, and it took a while for me to feel peaceful riding in a car again. Have you ever fallen off a bike and then were scared to get back on it again? When bad things happen, they can leave us feeling scared, worried, or even sad. God wants to heal your heart, so that you can get back out there and try again. He wants you to be able to live without being afraid something bad will happen. You can trust that His love will always keep you no matter what things come your way.

Sometimes unexpected things happen in your family, and you can't see them anymore. Maybe someone you love very much moved away or got really sick for a long time. Maybe a loved one even died. This can leave you sad or worried. Your heart can stay hurt for a long time, especially when things didn't turn out okay. Remember that we learned how God wants to heal our heart and soul. He can heal us from any hurt! The sooner you tell Jesus all about it, and give him your hurt and fear, the sooner your heart will be healed, and you will feel better.

He wants you to know that He is always with you, and that He can take the sadness away. He can strengthen you with His super dunamis power and fill you with hope and peace. He wants to comfort you with His love. You can talk to God about everything. Tell Him everything and let Him be there for you. Remember that His blood can heal your heart, and His super dunamis power can make you brave and strong again! God doesn't make bad things happen, but He will be there with you. And if you trust Him, He will work it out for good.

PRAYER

Thank You, God, that You are always there for me when bad things happen. With Your blood, please wash away the hurt in my heart from when

_____ happened.

Take away any fear, worry, hurt, or sadness, and fill me with Your super dunamis power, so that I can be brave, strong, peaceful, full of hope, and love again.

Jesus will always be with you.
He will always help you in times of trouble.

GOD HEALS MY HEART AND SOUL

CHAPTER 19- LESSONS FROM A GUY NAMED JOB- WHEN SATAN'S HELPERS BULLY US!

My dear children, you belong to God. So you have defeated them because God's Spirit, who is in you, is greater than the devil, who is in the world.
1 John 4:4 (ICB)

Bad things happen to everyone at some point. Sometimes it's good to know that you are not alone. We can learn a lot from a man in the Bible named Job.

Job was a man who loved God. He did good and turned away from evil. It sounds like the beginning of a good story, doesn't it? But do you remember earlier we talked about a bad guy, God's enemy, Satan, or sometimes called the devil? Well, here he is again trying to mess up Job's life. God's enemy, Satan, did not like Job and wanted to attack him so that he would turn away from God.

Did you know that God's enemy wanted to take God's place? He also convinced a lot of angels to follow him. These are Satan's helpers and they don't like God's people. They try to get people to turn away from God and serve God's enemy instead. But, no need to worry! God has all of His helpers, too. They are all the angels that stayed true to God. God's angels are very strong! They help and protect everyone who loves God.

There is no need to fear because our God is so much stronger than the enemy and all his helpers. God will always protect you, and will always win!

Did you know that Satan, who used to be called Lucifer, used to be one of God's angels? But, he chose to rebel against and disobey God.

Let's get back to Job's story.

In one day, Satan took everything that Job had. And if that wasn't enough, Satan attacked him with a sickness that gave him very painful sores all over his body. Job suffered many horrible things. All of this was very painful and hard to understand. It sure seemed like the enemy was winning, but Job still chose to trust God through all his troubles, and God sure came through for him! When it was all over, Job got back more than he had ever lost, and the Bible says that the second part of Job's life was much better than the life he had before all the trouble came. You can always trust that God is stronger than anything the enemy and his bullies try to do to you. God will always work it out for your good!

God is always with you. Even though Job trusted God, he still needed God to heal his heart. You see, even when we choose to trust God when bad things happen, our hearts can still get hurt. When we get bullied by Satan and his bullies, and bad things happen to us, God can heal our hearts too just like he healed Job's heart. Remember, the two best medicines, the blood of Jesus and His super power, dunamis, can heal us from anything that happens to us!

PRAYER

Thank You, God, that nothing can separate us from Your love! There is no trouble too big for You, and no enemy stronger than You, God! Thank you, God, that I can trust You to be greater than any enemy or bad thing I face! With your blood Jesus, please wash away the hurt in my soul, because it hurt when
_____ happened. Thank You, Jesus, for Your super power in me that is healing me of all the pain, hurt, sickness, fear, worry, or sadness I may feel. Thank you, Jesus, that You are always with me in trouble and working things out for my good!

LET'S CHECK IT OUT!
WHAT DOES THE BIBLE SAY?

"My dear children, you belong to God. So you have defeated them because God's Spirit, who is in you, is greater than the devil, who is in the world." 1 John 4:4 (ICB)

Read the verse above and fill in the blanks below.

God's Spirit is in _____.
The devil is in the _____.
God's Spirit is _____ than the devil.

"We know that in everything God works for the good of those who love him. They are the people God called, because that was his plan." Romans 8:28 (ICB)

Read the verse above and fill in the blanks below.

In_____ God works for the good of those who love Him.

EVERYTHING? Does that just mean the good things, or does it even mean the bad things too? _____

IT'S TIME FOR A CHECK UP

What is something special you have learned in this chapter, or from any part of this book so far? Write or draw a picture about it below.

GOD HEALS MY HEART AND SOUL

CHAPTER 20- SIN PASSED DOWN TO US

Don't punish us for the sins of our past sins. Show your mercy to us soon. We are helpless! God our Savior, help us so people will praise you. Save us and forgive our sins so people will honor you. Psalm 79:8-9 (ICB)

Has anyone looked at you and said that you look like your Mom or Dad? You have things that have been passed down to you from your parents like your looks, hair, smile, or eyes. Has anyone ever said that you act or do things just like your Mom or Dad? Maybe you laugh like them or enjoy the same things they do. Maybe you are kind and thoughtful or good at sports like they are. We all have things that are passed down to us from our parents. Sometimes these are good things, like patience or a friendly personality. We can also have faith, forgiveness, and blessings passed down to us too!

But sometimes things are passed down to us that are not so good, like a bad temper. Well, sin is one of those bad things that can get passed down to us from our parents. But thank God that it's not all bad, though. We get their good, too!

Go ahead and read the verse above again.

God is kind and forgives people for wrong and for turning against Him. But, some people don't want to ask God for forgiveness. They will still carry all that sin and hurt with them and pass it along to their family. Some of our family have just never known God's love or have been so hurt that it's hard for them to believe He will forgive them. We don't ever want to blame someone or point the finger at them. We always want to love them.

So, what can you do about any sin that may have been passed down to you from your family? The same thing you do for any other sin. You can ask God to forgive them, and for the blood of Jesus to wash away their sin, and any sin that they may have passed down to you. Ask God for His dunamis power to heal their souls and make them like Jesus! When you pray, God will wash away the sin and heal your family. It will definitely make a big difference in your life and theirs too!

The blood of Jesus and His super dunamis power
are the very best medicines you can apply.
They are powerful to wash every single sin away,
and heal any hurt in your soul!

PRAYER

God, thank You for my family. Thank You for my mom and dad! Thank You for all of the good – all of the blessings and love they have given to me! I honor my mom and dad! Jesus, I Thank You for Your blood that washes away all the sin that my family may have passed down to me. Thank You for healing their hearts and my heart too, for filling us up with Your super dunamis power, and helping us to be loving and a blessing to our families!

GOD HEALS MY BODY

CHAPTER 21- WHEN I GET SICK!

Jesus was teaching in one of the synagogues on the Sabbath day. In the synagogue there was a woman who had an evil spirit in her. This spirit had made the woman a cripple for 18 years. Her back was always bent; she could not stand up straight. When Jesus saw her, he called her over and said, "Woman, your sickness has left you!" Jesus put his hands on her. Immediately she was able to stand up straight and began praising God.
Luke 13:10-13 (ICB)

Did you know that sometimes when our hearts are hurting, they can make our bodies sick too? In the Bible verse above, we see a woman who was bent over and couldn't stand up straight. The verse above even tells us what was causing this – she had an evil spirit. When you study that word in the Bible, it is called an evil spirit of infirmity. Infirmity means to be sick not just in your soul, but in your body as well. So, that means one of Satan's bullies was making this woman sick in her soul and her body, which made her bent over with a physical disease in her body. This had been going on for a really long time - 18 years!

This woman lived during a time when Jesus was on the earth. Jesus saw this woman was sick and needed healing. He called the woman over to himself and set her free from the spirit of infirmity that was making her sick. The Bible says that she immediately stood up straight and glorified God. Jesus healed both her hurt soul and her sick body! Jesus can heal everything!

43

We don't need to fear any evil spirit or any of Satan's bullying helpers because, just like we see with this woman, Jesus has power over all of Satan's bullies! He can protect you, and He can free you from any of them that would try to bother you. Jesus is the healer of all of our sin, hurts, and sicknesses, whether they are caused by the enemy or not. Jesus is the answer. He is bigger and greater!

PRAYER

Thank You, Jesus, that You heal all of my hurts and my sicknesses.
Thank You that You are stronger than any of the enemy's bullies.
Thank You, Jesus, for healing any part of my heart that may be hurt and causing me to be sick. Thank You, Jesus, for setting me free from any bad spirit that may be making me sick. They must go in Jesus' name! Thank You for filling up my heart and my body with Your super dunamis power, making me strong and well!

SO, WHAT HAPPENED?

Now that you have read this chapter and Bible verse, answer the questions below.

How long was the woman sick?

_____

What was wrong with the woman's body?

_____

_____

What made the woman crippled for 18 years?

_____

_____

What did Jesus do when He saw the woman?

_____

_____

Fill in the blanks below.
Remember, when you studied about that evil spirit, it was a spirit of infirmity that made her sick in her soul and her body. So, that means Jesus healed her _____ and her _____ .

JESUS HEALS OUR SOUL AND OUR BODY.

BECOMING GOD'S SUPERHERO!

CHAPTER 22-HIS LIGHT HEALS US AND MAKES US LIKE JESUS!

But for you who revere my name, the sun of righteousness will rise with healing in its rays. And you will go out and frolic like well-fed calves.
Malachi 4:2 (NIV)

The sun in our world gives us light and shines bright. In the same way, God is full of light and shines on us! Not only that, but He shines on us with healing. That's right, healing! As we spend time with God, He shines on us and He heals us.

Have you ever been in the dark and felt scared? When bad things happen, or we have sinned, our hearts can hurt and we may feel lost, unsure, or confused, as if we were in the dark. It's hard to see in the dark, and that can be scary. It is easy to get confused and hard to find your way when it is dark. Well, that's how it is when your soul is hurt; you don't always understand what is happening, and you can get confused or feel scared. But there is good news! Jesus doesn't want you to stay hurt and in the dark. Jesus came with His light and shines it upon you so that you can know His healing.

When you turn on the light in your house, what happens to the darkness? That's right, it goes away! So anytime you are hurting and feel like you are in the dark, go to Jesus, tell Him everything, and He will turn on the light. Jesus will shine His light on you, heal your heart, and make all the darkness go away. Jesus is our light and darkness can't stay!

PRAYER

Thank You, Jesus, that You shine on me like the sun!
Thank You that You are healing me with Your light rays right now!
Jesus, You are light and make all the darkness go away!
The light of Jesus is shining into all of my heart, my mind and my body,
bringing healing to every part of me!

MIX AND MATCH

MATCH THE WORD ON THE LEFT WITH THE CORRECT
BLANK IN THE SENTENCE ON THE RIGHT.

darkness

God is light and He shines His
_____on us.

healing

There is _____ in the
rays of God's light or the "sun-beams"
of God's light.

light

As we spend time with God, He shines
His light on us and He _____
our heart and soul.

heals

When God shines His light on you, He
makes the _____
go away and heals your heart and soul.

BECOMING GOD'S SUPERHERO!

CHAPTER 23- SPENDING TIME WITH GOD AND BEING CHANGED!

*We can all draw close to him with the veil removed from our faces.
And with no veil we all become like mirrors who brightly reflect the glory of
the Lord Jesus. We are being transfigured (changed) into His very image as we move
from one brighter level of glory to another. And this glorious transfiguration (change)
comes from the Lord, who is the Spirit.*
2 Corinthians 3:18 (TPT)

Did you know that God wants to spend time with you? He sure does! As we spend time with God, His glory shines on us. Read the verse above. What does it say the Lord does when His glory shines on us? He makes us more and more like Him, and changes us into His image. You are like a mirror; when you spend time with God, you reflect Him! The glory of the Lord is something we can see and reflect! So, just like light shines and is reflected in a mirror, God's glory shines on us and reflects off of us. All of His glory, light, power, and love reflect off of us!

Not only that, but when we spend time with God, He shines His glory on us, and we are changed to become more and more like Him! Our heart and souls become like God's, full of His super dunamis power and glory, and we can love big like God. So, as we spend time with Him, His glory makes us like Him and heals us of any hurt that we may have. His glory heals us!

Sometimes you can actually feel God's glory. In the Bible there were times when the glory of God felt heavy like something pushing them down to the floor, so that they couldn't even get up. God's glory can come and cover you like a warm blanket and quiet you so much that you feel sleepy. Don't worry! Just let the Lord put you in a place of deep rest, so that He can heal your heart and soul. Sometimes it can give you goose bumps, make you feel all warm inside, or even cry good tears.

PRAYER

Thank You, God, that You like to spend time with me.
Thank You, God, for Your glory that is here right now and healing my soul!
Thank You for Your glory that makes me be like You –
full of light, glory, super dunamis power, and big love!

SPENDING TIME IN GOD'S GLORY

Sit back right where you are and close your eyes. Thank God that He is here and that He likes to spend time with you. Thank God for shining His light on you. Just sit quiet for a minute thinking about God and talking to Him. It may be easier to put on a worship song and just sit and be with God.

Did you hear God talking to you? Did God show you anything? If so, write or draw a picture about it.

BECOMING GOD'S SUPERHERO!

CHAPTER 24 - SPENDING TIME WITH GOD IN PRAYER!

People, trust God all the time. Tell him all your problems. God is our protection...
Psalm 62:8 (ICB)

When you spend time with your best friend, what do you do? Do you talk with them and tell them all about everything, both good and bad? It's the same with God; He wants to be your best friend. He wants you to talk with Him and tell Him everything, both good and bad. That's called prayer! Prayer is talking to God.

If you need help with something, who do you go to? Of course, our parents, teachers, and others can help us with many things, but there are some things only God can help with. For example, your parents and teachers can try to explain those hard math problems to you, but you may need God's help for your mind to understand them. God is always the best one to go to for help, because He will always be there for you. Going to God and asking Him for help is also prayer. God loves to help you and wants you to take all your needs to Him and ask Him for help. This is spending time with God too. And when you give God your needs, you give Him a chance to shine His light and His glory on it all, so that He can heal you and give you the help that you need.

When you talk to God in prayer, you are spending time with Him and allowing His glory and light to shine on you. God wants to fill up all of those places where you need help, with His light and glory, and give you the super dunamis power you need in every situation. He loves to do this for you! As you spend time with Him, His light and glory will fill you, and change you and your circumstances for good!

PRAYER

Thank You, Jesus, that You want to be my best friend!
Thank You that I can talk with You about anything!
As I spend time praying, You are shining Your light and Your glory on me!

ACTIVITY
LET'S TRY IT OUT

SPENDING TIME WITH GOD IN PRAYER!

Get somewhere you feel comfortable to speak out loud and talk to God. This is what prayer is. You can do this by yourself or with someone.

1. First, spend a minute or so thanking and praising God for all that He is and has done for you.

2. Then, spend a minute or so telling God what is on your heart, talking to Him like a friend.

3. Next, spend a minute or so asking God for what you need.

4. Then, spend a minute or so asking God for someone else's needs.

Thank you, God, that You hear all our prayers and You give us all that we need.

BECOMING GOD'S SUPERHERO!

CHAPTER 25- SPENDING TIME THANKING AND WORSHIPPING GOD!

Come into his city with songs of thanksgiving.
Come into his courtyards with songs of praise.
Thank Him, and praise His name.
Psalm 100:4 (ICB)

When somebody has been really nice to you or has really helped you, what do you do? Most of us thank them and let them know how much it means to us. Is there somebody you look up to and really admire? Don't you tell them how amazing they are and tell everybody all about them too?

Well, God has done more for us than anyone has! He is the greatest super hero of all time! He is always there for us. He does miracles and helps us all the time. He loved us so much, He died for us, forgives us, and heals our souls!

When we thank God for all that He has done for us and tell Him how amazing He is, that is worship! When we sing songs to God thanking and praising Him for all that He has done and for all that He will do, we are worshipping Him and spending time with Him. When we thank God and worship Him, His light and glory shines on us, heals our souls, and make us more and more like Him!

When we spend time worshipping God and praising Him, we are focusing our attention on Him and singing to Him. As we do this, we are spending time with Him, and using our hearts and minds to think about Him and look upon Him and His glory.

PRAYER

I thank You, God, for all that You have done for me and for how much You love me! Thank You, God, for _____! There is no one like You! I praise You for being so good to me, for loving me and _____.

ACTIVITY
👍 LET'S TRY IT OUT 👍

SPENDING TIME THANKING AND WORSHIPPING GOD

Get somewhere that you feel comfortable to talk and sing out loud to God. You can do this by yourself or with someone.

1. Spend a minute or so thanking God for all that He is and all that He has done for you.

2. Now, either turn on a worship song or just sing a song that you know or make up. Put your whole heart into it, and remember God is right there with you as you sing. Express your love and joy. You can clap, dance, lift your hands, or just sit quietly. He just loves to be with you!

BECOMING GOD'S SUPERHERO!

CHAPTER 26- SPENDING TIME WITH GOD IN HIS WORD!

All Scripture is inspired by God and is useful for teaching and for showing people what is wrong in their lives. It is useful for correcting faults and teaching how to live right.
2 Timothy 3:16 (ICB)

Have you ever received a letter in the mail or a card from someone? Usually, they write to tell you that they love you and the good things that they think about you. They also tell you all about themselves, and what they have done and are doing. Well, did you know that God has written a letter to you? It's a REALLY BIG ONE too! It's called the BIBLE. The Bible is God's letter to you. It tells us how much He loves us and what He thinks about us. It also tells us all about God – what He has done and what He is doing. When you read the Bible, your very own letter from God, you find out all about Him, what He has done, and what He is doing!

Reading the Bible is one of the best ways to get to know God and spend time with Him. And, you know what happens when you spend time with God? His glory and light shine on you! He heals you, makes you more like Him, and all the darkness, such as evil, fear, and confusion, runs away from you! Spending time with God reading His Word each day, is so important. Let His light and glory shine in your life!

When we spend time reading God's Word, thinking about it, learning it, and focusing on it, God's Word does amazing things in our life! Then, when we speak and pray God's Word, it does powerful things! The Bible tells us so much about what God's Word does for us. It will make the things happen in our lives, that God wants to see happen. It can keep us from sinning. It gives light and helps us understand. And, we know that God's light brings healing, so if God's Word is light then it heals our souls too! God's Word comforts us and gives life.

PRAYER
Thank You, God, for loving us so much that
You wrote us one big letter in the Bible.
Thank You for Your Word that changes me and gives me light!
Thank You, God, that as I remember Your Word, it helps me know what to do.

SPENDING TIME IN GOD'S WORD

Go get a Bible and get somewhere comfortable. You can do this by yourself or with someone else.

1. Find Matthew 19: 13-15. If you aren't sure how to find this in the Bible, ask someone to help you. The Bible is made up of lots of tiny books. This Bible passage is in the book of Matthew, chapter 19, in the verses 13-15.

2. Pray and ask God to open your heart to understand. Now go ahead and read Matthew 19:13-15.

3. Write below what you learned about Jesus.

_____
_____
_____
_____

4. This section was about children and I'm pretty sure only children are reading this book (not dinosaurs ☺). So, if you are a child too, what does this part of the Bible tell you about you?

_____
_____
_____
_____

BECOMING GOD'S SUPERHERO!

CHAPTER 27- GOD'S SUPER POWER MAKES ME GREAT!

I pray that out of His glorious riches He may strengthen you with power through His Spirit in your inner being.
Ephesians 3:16 (NIV)

This is a great prayer that you can pray too! You can ask God to strengthen you with power through His Spirit on the inside of you, in your heart and soul. Do you remember that we talked about God's super dunamis power? Well, this is that same power that raised Jesus from the dead, and it is inside of you! It is powerful, and it is strengthening you from the inside out. This power heals your heart and soul, making you strong, well, and happy. It gives you the power on the inside to be super heroes like Jesus was on the earth, so that your heart can be as strong and amazing as His heart. Jesus loved everyone, even those that were mean to him. This power will help you to love and forgive, even when people aren't nice to you. It will give you patience and kindness.

This power is always at work inside of you, and it will give you a heart just like Jesus'. All that you need to do is ask! When you ask God to fill you up with this super dunamis power, you can be sure that He will. If you are struggling to sit still in school, just ask God's super power to fill you up, and help you to have self-control and to be at peace. Whatever you may be struggling with on the inside, whether you are sad, mad, or just want to give up, you always have a big tankful of God's super power inside of you, that you can use just by asking God to fill you up. You don't need to wait till you need help either; you can ask God to fill you up with His super dunamis power every day as much as you want! The more you do, the more you will have an amazing super hero heart like Jesus!

PRAYER

Thank You, God, that Your super power is strengthening me on the inside! I am being filled up with Your super power right now, and it is making my heart and soul excellent just like Jesus'! Thank You for filling me with love, joy, peace, patience, kindness, goodness, faithfulness, gentleness, and self-control.

ACTIVITY
LET'S BE GOD'S SUPERHEROES!

GET IN A PLACE THAT IS COMFORTABLE SO THAT YOU CAN SPEAK OUT LOUD TO GOD.

1. Think for a moment: What do you need God's super dunamis power for? It could be something that is making you feel mad, sad, or scared, something you are having a hard time with, or a sin you need help overcoming.

2. Choose just one thing right now and think about what it will be like when God's super dunamis power comes in, changes it, and makes you great!
Write it down below.

_____
_____
_____

3. Now, using your voice, thank God for doing all that you thought of above. Thank You, God, that Your super dunamis power is making me great!
Your super dunamis power in me, is changing _____.
Your super dunamis power is working in me, and doing more than I can ask or imagine!

Thank You, God, that Your super dunamis power is making me great! Your super dunamis power in me is changing

_____
_____
_____.

BECOMING GOD'S SUPERHERO!

CHAPTER 28- GOD'S SUPER POWER IN ME HEALS THE SICK!

Jesus called the twelve apostles together.
He gave them power to heal sicknesses and power over all demons.
Jesus sent the apostles out to tell about God's kingdom and to heal the sick.
Luke 9:1-2 (ICB)

Jesus wasn't the only one to heal people using God's super dunamis power. He gave it to His disciples too, and it gave them power to do signs, wonders, and miracles. Jesus gives you His power and you can do the same! If you believe in Jesus, you are His disciple and follower too. So, what does Jesus want you to do with the power that He gives you? He not only wants you to be healed, but for you to give His power away, and pray for others that are sick too.

Remember, we get our word dynamite from the Greek word "dunamis".
It is super powerful, so taking care of sickness is easy!

Sometimes sickness is caused by Satan's bullies. Sometimes it can be caused by our hearts being sick. Other times, we may have just eaten something bad. No matter what, God's super dunamis power can help you overcome Satan's bullies, heal your heart, and heal your body. What an amazing gift! You have dunamis power too. You just need to use it! Everyone who believes in Jesus has this super dunamis power inside. But, just like a gift that sits on a shelf unwrapped, some people never use it. All you need to do is open it up and use that super dunamis power that is inside you. Put it to work to heal yourself and others, just like Jesus did. Send the super dunamis power to your body or to your friends that are sick and need healing. So, let's put it to work!

PRAYER

Thank You, Jesus, for Your super dunamis power inside of me that heals my heart and my body! I thank You for Your blood that washes me of any sin and sickness. I am filled with super dunamis power and it is healing anything in my heart and body that is not well right now. I pray for Your blood to wash away any sin and sickness in my friends or family that are sick. I send Your super dunamis power to _____ so that You will fill them up and heal them. Thank You that there is never an end to Your super dunamis power! I can fill up and send it out all day long and it will never run out!

ACTIVITY
LET'S BE GOD'S SUPERHEROES!

God's super dunamis power makes us bold and brave!! Let's give out what God has freely given us! Is there someone that you know who is sick or hurt and needs God's super dunamis power to heal them?

1. Pray for them each day and ask God for a chance to actually pray for them in person.

2. The next time you see them, try asking them if you could pray for them. If they aren't comfortable, then just keep praying for them on your own. God always hears your prayers, even if it takes a while to know His answers. Don't give up!

BECOMING GOD'S SUPERHERO!

CHAPTER 29– GOD'S SUPER POWER IN ME DOES MIRACLES!

...He gave them power to drive out evil spirits and to heal every kind of disease and sickness... Heal the sick. Give dead people life again.
Heal those who have harmful skin diseases. Force demons to leave people.
I give you these powers freely. So help other people freely.
Matthew 10:1, 8 (ICB)

You have a huge tankful of God's super dunamis power inside you, and it gives you the power to heal the sick and do miracles, just like Jesus did. This is the same power that raised Jesus from the dead! I know it may seem hard to believe, but Jesus raised people from the dead. He Himself rose from the dead and He gives you the power to do that too! It sounds impossible doesn't it? But, you can do all things through Jesus who strengthens you! What is impossible with us, is possible with God and His super dunamis power at work in us!

Jesus did many miracles when He was on earth. He took five loaves of bread and two fish and multiplied them so that 5000 people could eat! That seems impossible, right? But Jesus did that miracle, and you can too! When the disciples needed money to pay a bill, He made money appear in a fish's mouth! You don't have to look very hard to find someone you know that needs a miracle. A miracle is something God does that seems like it is impossible to do, but God does it. God freely gives us His love, His forgiveness, and His power. He wants us to freely give His love, forgiveness, and power too, to heal the sick and do miracles just like Jesus did. Other people may not know Jesus as well as you do, but they can get to know Him as you give what He has freely given you.

Through the super dunamis power of Jesus, you too can heal the sick, raise the dead, and do miracles! His power can do miracles through you, and through you this power can heal the hearts and bodies of others too!

PRAYER

Thank You, Jesus, for Your super power that is inside of me! I believe that You gave me this super dunamis power so that I too can do miracles just like You did! Thank You for freely giving me this power so that I can see miracles in my life. Help me to be brave so that I freely use this power to see miracles and healing in other people's lives too! Help me to see my friends that need a miracle, and give them what Jesus gave me! I pray for Your super dunamis power to do a miracle for _____ because they need _____. Thank You that Your super dunamis power will do a miracle in their life and mine!

ACTIVITY

👍 LET'S BE GOD'S SUPERHEROES! 👍

God's super dunamis power makes us bold and brave! Let's give out what God has freely given us! Is there someone you know that needs a miracle? Do you know someone that needs God's super dunamis power to do something for them that seems really hard or impossible?

1. Pray for them each day and ask God for a chance to actually pray for them in person.

2. The next time you see them, try asking them if you could pray for them. If they aren't comfortable, then just keep praying for them on your own. God always hears your prayers even if it takes a while for you to see an answer, so don't give up!

BECOMING GOD'S SUPERHERO!

CHAPTER 30- GOD'S SUPER POWER IN ME IS STRONGER THAN SATAN'S BULLIES!

...He gave them power to drive out evil spirits and to heal every kind of disease and sickness... Heal the sick. Give dead people life again. Heal those who have harmful skin diseases. Force demons to leave people. I give you these powers freely. So help other people freely.
Matthew 10:1, 8 (ICB)

Let's take a look at one more thing God's super power does for you. The verse above says that it gives you power to "force demons to leave people". The word demon is just another name for Satan's helpers or bullies. They are our enemies. God, who lives inside you, is greater than anything in this world that you may face, including demons. From earlier chapters, we know that Satan's helpers can cause lots of trouble in our lives, even making us sick, but the good news is that God's super power that is inside you is stronger! This power is able to force demons to leave people, and all you need to do to get this power working, is say the name of Jesus. So just say, "In the name of Jesus, you demons need to leave."

If you ever feel like you are being bullied by Satan's helpers, just ask Jesus if there is any sin in your life, that you might not be aware of, that might give the enemy a little power in your life.

God is so faithful to show you if there is any sin.

Then tell Jesus you are sorry for your sin, and ask Him to cleanse you with His blood. He will be faithful to take all your sin away! Then, thank Him for filling you up with His super dunamis power. Then, say to the enemy, "You now have no power here. Go in the name of Jesus!"

PRAYER

If there is any sin in my heart that may be giving the enemy power in my life, please show it to me so that I can give it to You to wash me clean. (Now, just listen and give that sin to Jesus, if there is any. If not, just continue praying.) Jesus, thank You for Your blood that washes away all my sin, and thank You that You have given me Your super power! Thank You, Jesus, for the power You give us over the enemy! Thank You that, in Your name, the enemy must go! So now, in Jesus' name, I tell any evil spirit to go, now! Thank You, Jesus, for making the enemy go, and for filling me up with Your super dunamis power. Thank You for healing anything the enemy may have hurt in my life!

LET'S GET THINGS STRAIGHT!

Read the Bible verses and fill in the blanks below.

1. In James 4:7 (ICB), the Bible says, "So give yourselves to God. Stand against the devil, and the devil will run away from you."

So, when you feel bullied by the devil (our enemy), what do you need to do?

I need to _____myself to God. _____against the devil, and the devil will _____ away from me.

2. "You, dear children, are from God and have overcome them, because the one who is in you is greater than the one who is in the world."
1 John 4:4 (NIV)

I am from God, and God who is in me, is _____ than the enemy in the world!

3. "... He gave them power to drive out evil spirits and to heal every kind of disease and sickness." Matthew 10:1 (ICB)

Jesus gives me _____ to drive out evil spirits, and to heal every kind of disease and sickness!

IT'S TIME FOR A CHECK UP!

What special thing did you learn in this chapter, or from any part of the book so far?
Be sure to tell about something other than what you shared on page 40.
Write or draw a picture about it below.

HEART AND SOUL DECREES

CHAPTER 31- SPEAK AND DECREE GOD'S WORD!

You shall (will) also decide and decree a thing, and it shall (will) be established (or done) for you; and the light [of God's favor] shall (will) shine upon your ways.
Job 22:28 (AMPC)

Let's learn a new word. It is "decree". To decree means we just take the verses in God's Word, make them personal (make them about us), and speak them out! God's Word is always true! So, when we speak God's Word, we are speaking what is true, it heals our soul, and completes God's purpose in our lives.

"Established" is a big word and has a big meaning. It means that it will be done for you. When we decree God's Word in our lives, it is powerful! It will do what it says, so that very thing that you decree and speak out will be done for you. Now that is powerful!

So, let's try making a decree together, starting with the Bible verse above. Now let's make this into a decree! We'll make it mean something to us, and speak it out!

DECREE

Thank You, God, that as I speak out Your Word, it will be done for me! Thank You that as I speak out Your Word, Your light will shine on me! Your light brings me healing! As I decree Your Word, You will cause Your purpose and plans to be done in my life!

Let's make the following Bible verses into decrees. I'll help you out a little.

1. **Bible Verse:**
   We know that in everything God works for the good of those who love him… Romans 8:28 (ICB)

   Decree:
   I know that in everything God works for my
   _____ because I _____ Him!

2. **Bible Verse:**
   With God's power working in us, God can do much, much more than anything we can ask or think of. Ephesians 3:20 (ICB)

   Decree:
   God, with Your _____working in me, You can do much, much more than anything _____ can ask or think of!

3. **Bible Verse:**
   But for you who revere my name, the sun of righteousness will rise with healing in its rays… Malachi 4:2 (NIV)

   Decree:
   I revere and worship You, Jesus! You are like the
   _____. You rise and shine upon me with
   _____ in Your rays of light! I am healed
   in Your light!

HEART AND SOUL DECREES

CHAPTER 32- DECREE GOD'S SUPER DUNAMIS POWER INTO OUR LIVES!

TO TURN ON THE SUPER DUNAMIS POWER IN ME!

The dunamis power that raised Jesus from the dead is inside of me, and I release it into my soul, body, and the lives of people around me. (Romans 8:11)

GOD'S SUPER DUNAMIS POWER LIVES IN ME!

My body is the temple of God. God's Spirit lives inside of me. He has made His home inside of me. His spirit is full of dunamis power and His dunamis power lives inside of me. (1 Corinthians 6:19)

GOD'S SUPER DUNAMIS POWER MAKES ME LIKE JESUS!

With God's dunamis power inside of me, I am able to be like Jesus! He makes me more and more like Him when I spend time with Him. (2 Corinthians 3:18)

GOD'S SUPER DUNAMIS POWER MAKES MY SOUL EXCELLENT, JUST LIKE JESUS!

I am filled with God's dunamis power that makes my soul excellent, just like Jesus'! Thank You for filling me with love, joy, peace, patience, kindness, goodness, faithfulness, gentleness, and self-control! (Galatians 5:22)

GOD'S SUPER DUNAMIS POWER SHUTS THE DOOR ON SIN AND MAKES EVIL RUN AWAY!

Through God's power in me, I am able to stand against evil and shut the door on sin. Evil will run away! (James 4:7)

GOD'S SUPER DUNAMIS POWER IN ME, DOES MORE THAN I CAN ASK OR IMAGINE!

I thank You, God, that Your dunamis power is working inside of me, and is able to do more than I can ask, think, or imagine! (Ephesians 3:19-20)

GOD'S SUPER DUNAMIS POWER MAKES ME STRONG!

I am strengthened with His mighty dunamis power. When I am weak, He is strong! (Ephesians 3:16)

HEART AND SOUL DECREES

CHAPTER 33- DECREES FOR THE LIGHT AND GLORY OF GOD!

FOR GOD'S GLORY TO FILL EVERY PART OF ME!
I lift up the gates of every part of my soul and body. Jesus, the King of Glory, come in and heal every wound within me by the power of Your glory!
(Psalm 24:7)

FOR JESUS TO SHINE ON ME WITH HEALING!
I thank You, Jesus, the Sun of Righteousness, that You are rising upon me with healing in Your wings. Your light is shining on me and Your glory is healing all parts of my body, any hurt feelings or bad thoughts, and giving me the ability to make good choices. I am being healed in Your light! (Malachi 4:2)

FOR SAFETY AND PROTECTION IN HIS WINGS!
God, Your love is so precious! You protect me as a bird protects her young under her wings. I am safe with You! (Psalm 36:7, Psalm 91)

WHEN I WANT TO FEEL THAT GOD IS WITH ME, I PRAISE HIM!
I thank You, God, that You live in the praises of Your people. I praise You, God, and I know that You are with me because You live in my praises. (Psalm 22:3)

WHEN I DON'T UNDERSTAND, YOU HELP ME UNDERSTAND!
I thank You, God, that when I can't understand things, You give me light and help me understand correctly. (John 8:12, James 1:5-7)

WHEN I DON'T KNOW WHAT TO DO, YOU SHOW ME!
I thank You, God, that when I have trouble seeing where to go or what to do in a situation, You are My light and You show me where to go and what to do.
(John 14:6, Psalm 119:105)

HEART AND SOUL DECREES

CHAPTER 34 – DECREES THAT HEAL WHEN WE SIN OR GET HURT!

WHEN I SIN

I come to You, Jesus, to tell You that when I made a bad choice and did this:_____, I sinned.
I thank You that You forgive me of every sin and that Your blood washes me clean of every sin. Your super dunamis power is changing me so that I won't do that again. (1 John 1:9)

WHEN I GET HURT AND SOMEONE SINS AGAINST ME

I come to You Jesus, to tell You that when this happened:_____
_____, it hurt me, and made me
feel _____.

I thank You that You died on the cross to take this hurt and pain away, so I give it to You. I thank You that You heal my broken heart. I choose to forgive _____ for what they did to me, because You forgive me of my sins (Isaiah 53:4, Matthew 6:14). Thank You for Your blood washing away the sin and hurt in my soul, and for Your super dunamis power that is healing me now!

I know that this person hurt me because they are hurting and need You too. Please heal their heart. I pray they know Your love more. I pray for You to bless them. (Luke 6:28)

HEART AND SOUL DECREES

CHAPTER 35- DECREES THAT HEAL WHEN BAD THINGS HAPPEN!

DECREES THAT HEAL WHEN BAD THINGS HAPPEN

When something happens that makes me afraid, Jesus, I come to You because I know that You love me. When _____ happened, it made me feel afraid. I thank You that Your blood is washing away all hurt, and You are healing my soul with Your super dunamis power. You fill every part of me with Your love and make fear leave, because Your perfect love takes away fear. (1 John 4:18)

WHEN SOMETHING HAPPENS, AND I AM AFRAID TO DO THINGS

Jesus, I come to You because You make me bold and strong. When _____ happened it caused me to never want to do _____ again. Thank You for Your blood washing away all hurt, fear, and my sin of not trusting You. I thank You, God, that I can trust You to protect me, and if something that seems bad comes, I will trust You to work it out for my good. I can do all things through Jesus who strengthens me. You give me Your super dunamis power, love, and a strong mind! (Romans 8:28, 2 Timothy 1:7)

WHEN SOMETHING HAPPENS AND I CAN'T STOP THINKING OF IT

Jesus, You restore me and make me new. Since _____ happened, I continue to think about it, and feel hurt all over again. I thank You that You are my healer. Let the blood of Jesus wash away the hurt and pain. You make my mind new, and help me forget the pain and memory of what happened. Thank You that You fill my mind with good thoughts, and my soul with Your super dunamis power, making them full of joy and peace. (Psalm 23:3, Romans 12:2, Ephesians 4:23, Psalm 147:3, Philippians 4:8)

Jesus, I come to You because You care for me and hear my prayers. Since _____ happened, I worry every time _____. Well, you told me not to worry about ANYTHING, but to pray and ask You to help. So, I give this worry to You! Forgive me for worrying, and wash me with Your blood. Thank You for Your super dunamis power strengthening my soul to trust that You are taking care of this, and protecting me. You provide all of my needs. You love and care for the people in my life, and can help them even better than I can. Lord, I trust You and receive Your peace. (Philippians 4:6-7)

HEART AND SOUL DECREES

CHAPTER 36- DECREES TO HELP ME...

WHEN I FEEL WEAK, YOU ARE STRONG!

I praise You, God, that You are strong and mighty and that when I feel weak, You are strong!
(2 Corinthians 12:9-10)

WHEN I NEED COMFORT, YOU COMFORT ME!

I praise You that You are the God of all comfort! When I am sad or upset, You love to comfort me and love me.
(2 Corinthians 1:3)

WHEN I AM IN NEED, YOU PROVIDE!

I praise You, Jesus, that You provide all my needs with all of Your riches in glory (heaven). When it feels like I don't have enough (friends, ability, things, help, money, love, etc.) I trust that You will fill me and my life with all that I need.
(Philippians 4:19)

WHEN I AM IN TROUBLE, YOU ARE WITH ME!

I praise You Jesus that You are always with me in trouble. You will never leave me or forget me.

(Psalm 46:1, Deuteronomy 31:6)

WHEN I AM WORRIED AND AFRAID, YOU TAKE CARE OF ME!

I praise and thank You, God, that You take care of me. You are My Good Shepherd. I don't need to fear because You protect me. I don't need to worry because You always care for me.

(Psalm 23, 1 Peter 5:7)

WHEN I AM STRUGGLING WITH SIN, YOU MAKE ME LIKE YOU!

I praise You and thank You that You change me and make me like You – good, loving peaceful, patient, gentle, kind, honest, and with self-control. Thank You that as I look to You, You change me little by little to become more like You.

(2 Corinthians 3:18, Galatians 5:22)

WHEN I FEEL LIKE I'M FAILING, YOU MAKE ME A CONQUEROR!

I won't keep losing my battles; You help me win! You help me conquer things that are too big for me. When it feels like I keep failing, You show me the way to victory!

(Romans 8:37, 2 Corinthians 2:14)

WHEN I DON'T FEEL SPECIAL OR LOVED, YOU LOVE ME!

I thank You, God, that when I don't feel special or loved, You tell me that I am precious, I am chosen by You, I am Your child, and I am special. You loved me so much that You gave Your life for me.

(Isaiah 43:4, 1 Peter 2:9, John 1:12, Galatians 2:20)

NOTES AND JOURNALING

A journal is a place for you to write about things that you experience. Use these pages to write anything that you would like about your experiences, as you learn more about the Lord through reading this book.

NOTES AND JOURNALING

NOTES AND JOURNALING

NOTES AND JOURNALING

ENDNOTES

1 – (Dictionary and Word Search for "live")(Strong's G3811), Strong's Concordance, Blue Letter Bible. https://www.blueletterbible.org/lang/Lexicon/Lexicon.cfm?strongs=G2198&t=KJV

2 – (Dictionary and Word Search for "save") (Strong's G4982). Strong's Concordance, Blue Letter Bible. https://www.blueletterbible.org/lang/Lexicon/Lexicon.cfm?strongs=G4982&t=KJV